What We Have in Common

Brim Coloring Book
Written by Jane Landey
Edited by David Austin
Drawings by David Austin and Jane Austin

Copyright©2017

Published by CreateSpace: An Amazon Company
Printed in U.S.A.

Introduction

What We Have in Common Brim Books display the similarities of related animals. In this series, the starfish and the octopus are compared. The facts enable children to appreciate common values. Thus, imbibing in them interest towards animals which could make them to appreciate what they have in common with one another.

The Starfish

And

The Octopus

Starfish and Octopus are sea
animals. They have several limbs and
live in water.

The starfish and the octopus meet in the sea.

I am a starfish.

I am an octopus.

I live in the sea.

I live in the sea too!

I have five hands.

I have many hands too!

I eat tiny fish.

I eat tiny fish too!

I love to eat weeds.

I love to eat weeds too!

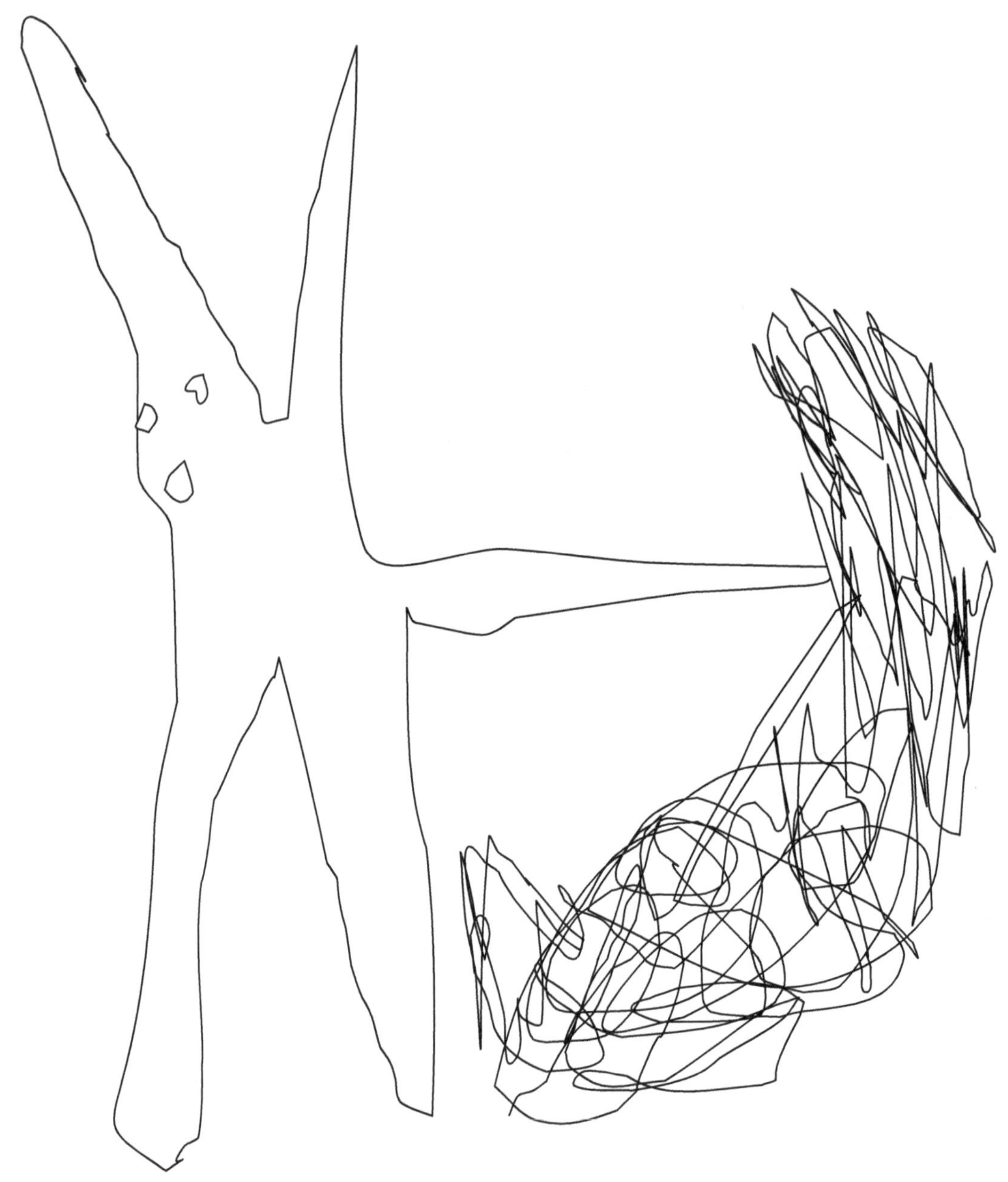

I drink lots of water.

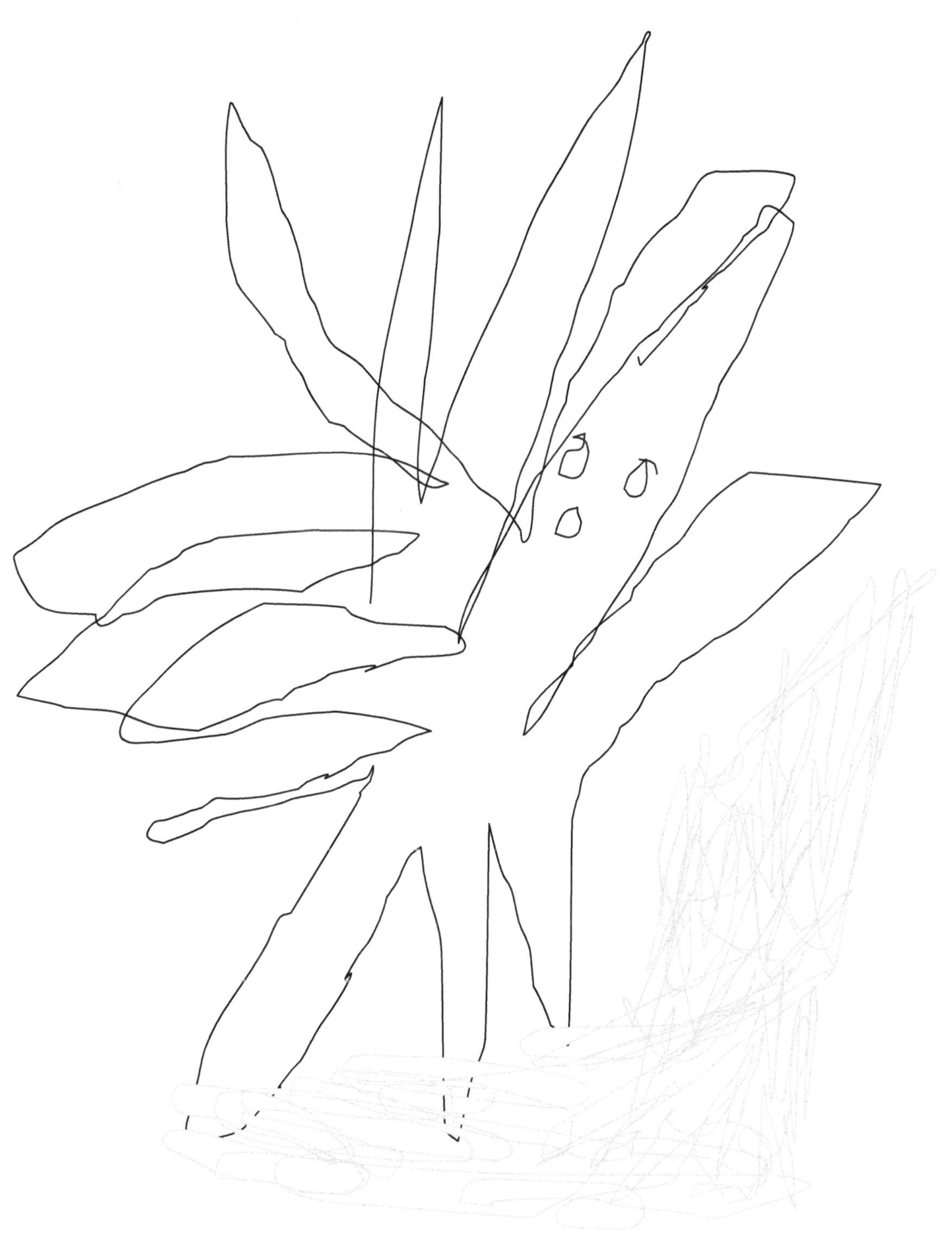

I drink lots of water too!

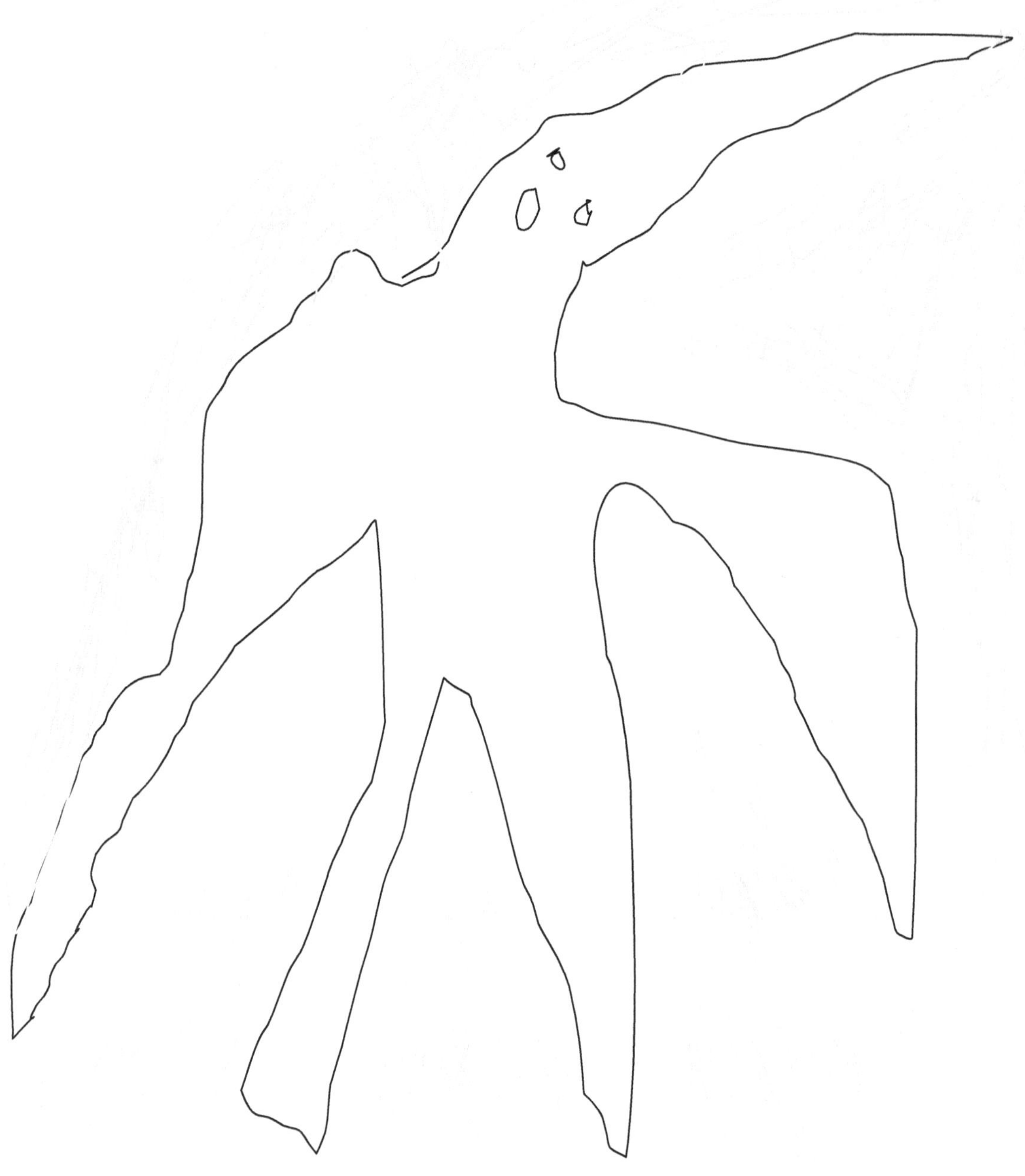

I play in deep water.

So do I!

I can swim.

I can swim too!

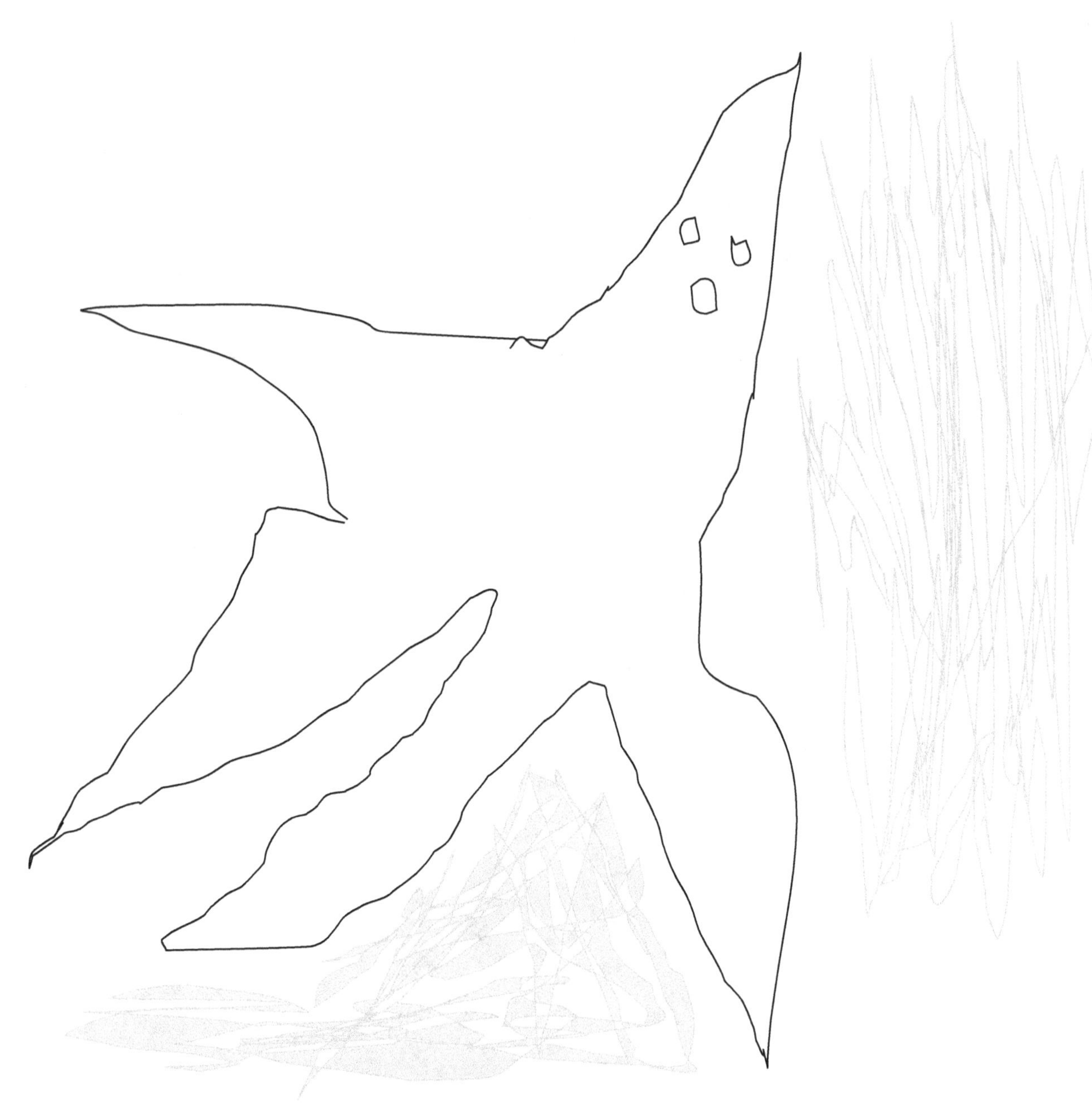

I can search the deep.

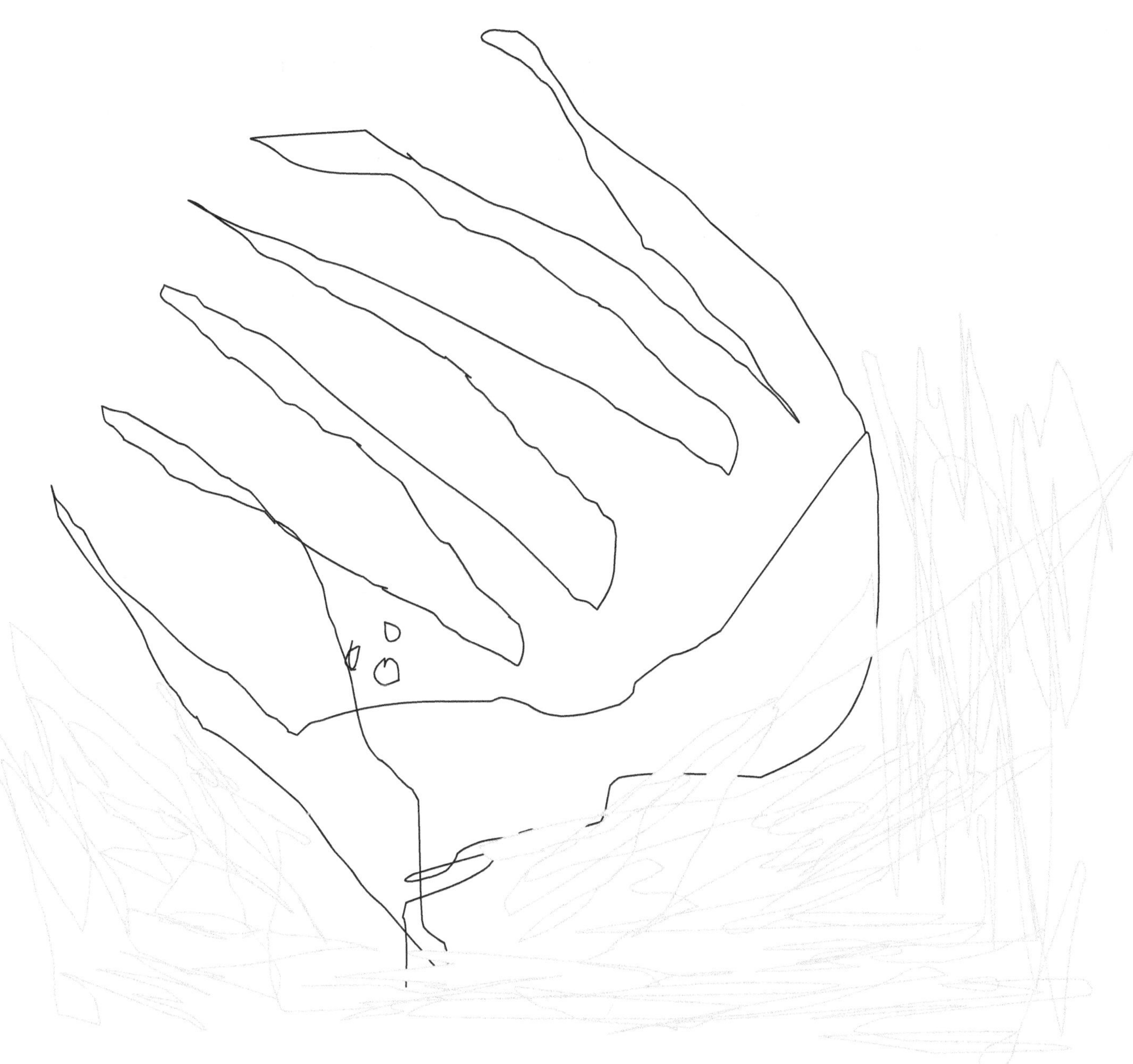

Let's go look for fish! Do you want to
go?

Of course yes!

I will go home with you!

I live down the sea.

I want to see your home!

I can dance with my fingers.

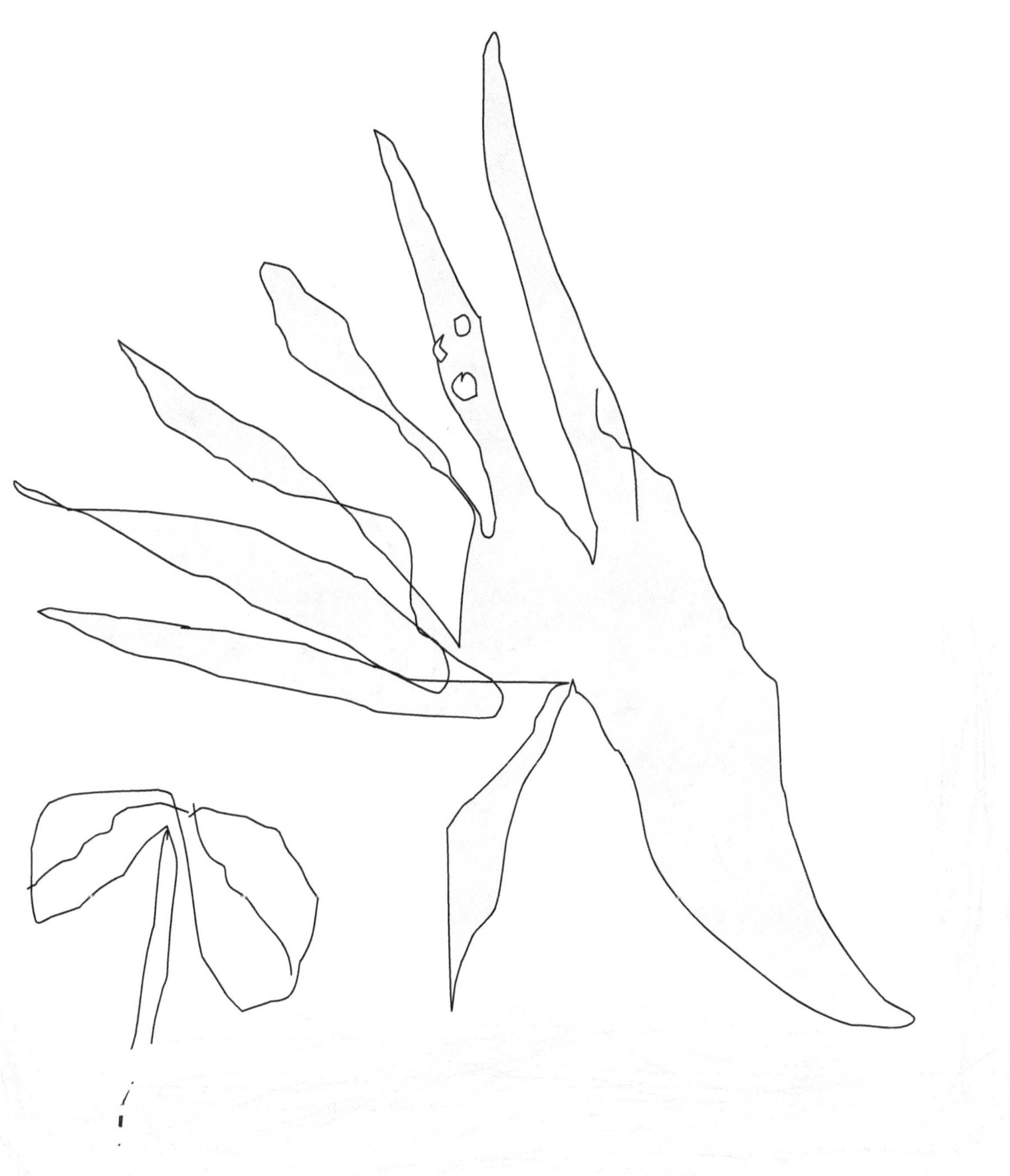

So do I!

There are corals and pearls in my
home!

I must take some back home!

Are you ready to go with me?

Yes I am!

Alright let us go!

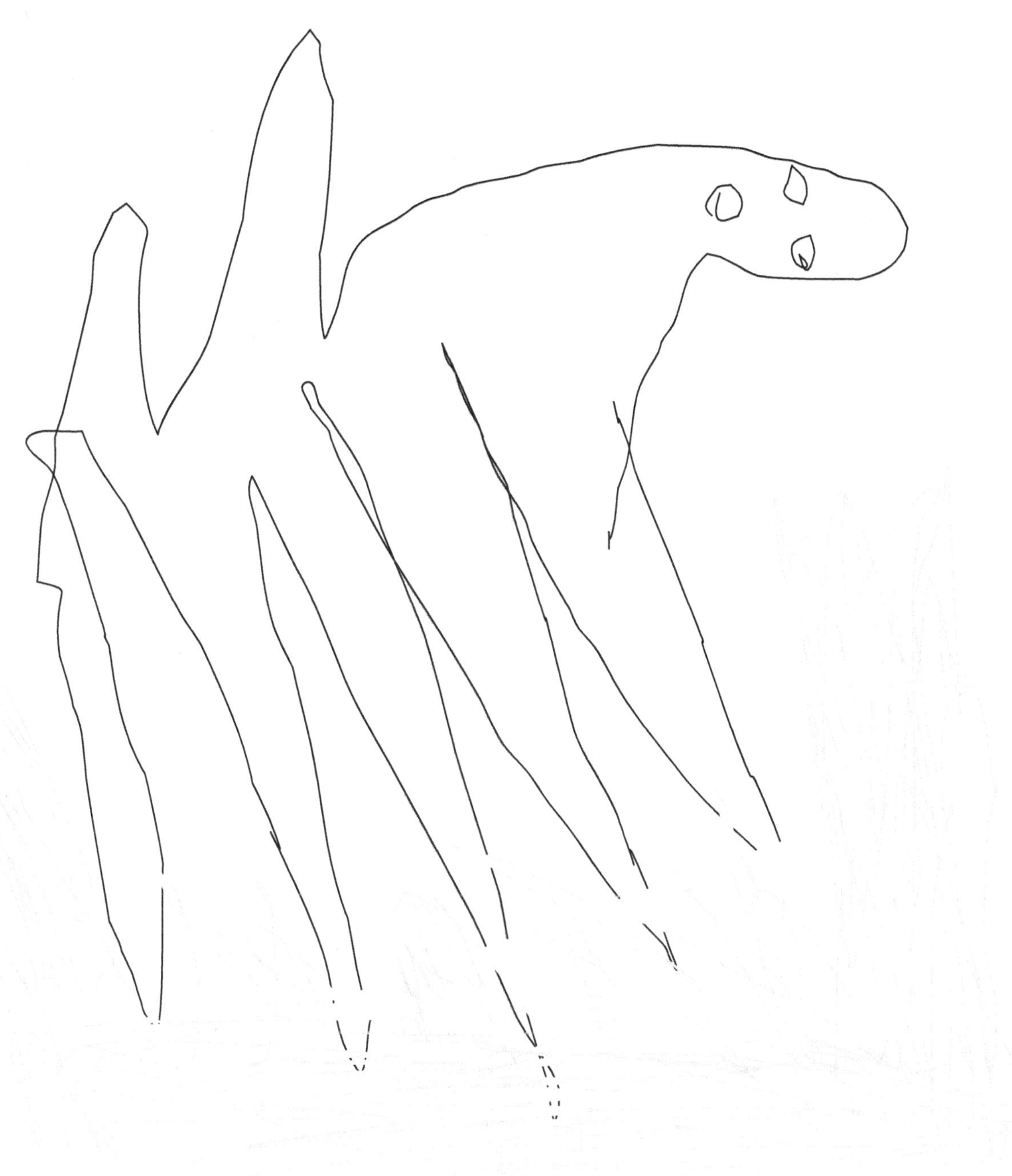

Are we almost there?

Take as many as you want!

What We Have in Common Brim Coloring Books

Crocodile and Alligator
Turtle and Tortoise
Starfish and Octopus
Worm and Snake
Turkey and Vulture
Ostrich and Emu
Weka and Kiwi
Bat and Rat
Camel and Llama
Duck and Pelican
Kangaroo and Wallaby
Pig and Tapir
Skunk and Squirrel
Hedge and Anteater
Cat and Owl
Elephant and Rhinoceros
Dog and fox
Buffalo and Bull
Leopard and Cheetah
Horse and Zebra